TABLE OF CONTENTS

Workbook Answers

Chapter 1 - Place Value and Number Sense

Pg 6

Draw the shape that comes next in the pattern.

1. ○ ○ □ □ △ △
2. □ □ □ ○ ○ ○
3. □ △ ○ □ △ ○ □ △ ○
4. △ △ △ ○ ○ ○ □ □ □
5. ⬠ □ △ ⬠ □ △ ⬠
6. △ ▽ □ □ △ ▽
7. ⬠ ⬠ ⬠ △ △ △ ○ ○ ○
8. ⬠ □ △ ⬠ □ △ ⬠ □

Pg 7			
No.	Answer	No.	Answer
1	even	13	odd
2	odd	14	even
3	even	15	even
4	even	16	even
5	odd	17	odd
6	even	18	odd
7	odd	19	even
8	odd	20	even
9	even	21	odd
10	odd	22	odd
11	odd	23	even
12	even	24	even

- 4 -

Pg 8		Pg 9		Pg 10		Pg 11	
No.	Answer	No.	Answer	No.	Answer	No.	Answer
1	odd	1	300	1	8,000	1	78
2	even	2	900	2	1,000	2	34
3	even	3	300	3	2,000	3	15
4	odd	4	100	4	9,000	4	2
5	odd	5	200	5	1,000	5	8
6	even	6	800	6	6,000	6	9
7	odd	7	800	7	4,000	7	3
8	even	8	100	8	9,000	8	5
9	even	9	800	9	2,000	9	89
10	even	10	400	10	7,000		
11	odd	11	300	11	2,000		
12	odd	12	300	12	5,000		
13	even	13	600	13	7,000		
14	odd	14	1,000	14	4,000		
15	odd	15	200	15	7,000		
16	even	16	300	16	9,000		
17	even	17	400	17	1,000		
18	even	18	700	18	5,000		
19	even	19	700	19	5,000		
20	even	20	500	20	2,000		
21	odd	21	200	21	2,000		
22	odd	22	800	22	1,000		
23	odd	23	300	23	2,000		
24	even	24	200	24	5,000		
		25	800	25	1,000		
		26	200	26	9,000		
		27	800	27	8,000		
		28	300	28	3,000		

Pg 12		Pg 13		Pg 14	
No.	Answer	No.	Answer	No.	Answer
1	24	1	129	1	1,347
2	43	2	235	2	3,232
3	39	3	254	3	2,459
4	66	4	325	4	4,157
5	59	5	507	5	3,175
6	86				

Pg 15	
No.	Answer
1	4,818 | 4,982 | 14,818
2	880 | 1,251 |1,900
3	1,210 | 1,541 | 1,780
4	50 | 74 | 129
5	815 | 1,520 | 3,500
6	3,400 | 5,800 | 9,570
7	10 | 100 | 1,000
8	5 | 300 | 4,500
9	250 | 275 | 300
10	16 | 25 | 54

Pg 16		Pg 17		Pg 18	
No.	Answer	No.	Answer	No.	Answer
1	>	1	>	1	1,221
2	>	2	<	2	2,142
3	<	3	=	3	333
4	<	4	>	4	3,321
5	<	5	>	5	2,340
6	=	6	>		
7	=	7	<		
8	<	8	<		
9	>	9	=		
10	<	10	<		
11	>	11	>		
12	<	12	<		
13	>	13	>		
14	=	14	=		
15	>	15	<		
16	>	16	<		
17	<	17	=		
18	=	18	>		
19	<	19	>		
20	<	20	<		

Pg 19

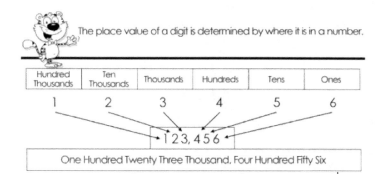

The place value of a digit is determined by where it is in a number.

Hundred Thousands	Ten Thousands	Thousands	Hundreds	Tens	Ones
1	2	3	4	5	6

123,456

One Hundred Twenty Three Thousand, Four Hundred Fifty Six

Write these numbers correctly in the blanks.

1. 392,599 =

3	9	2	5	9	9
Hundred Thousands	Ten Thousands	Thousands	Hundreds	Tens	Ones

2. 415,675 =

4	1	5	6	7	5
Hundred Thousands	Ten Thousands	Thousands	Hundreds	Tens	Ones

3. 726,211 =

7	2	6	2	1	1
Hundred Thousands	Ten Thousands	Thousands	Hundreds	Tens	Ones

4. 186,452 =

1	8	6	4	5	2
Hundred Thousands	Ten Thousands	Thousands	Hundreds	Tens	Ones

Chapter 2 – Addition

Pg 21		Pg 22		Pg 23	
No.	**Answer**	**No.**	**Answer**	**No.**	**Answer**
1	79	1	121	1	166
2	89	2	47	2	134
3	62	3	89	3	138
4	77	4	84	4	131
5	99	5	113	5	55
6	106	6	94	6	165
7	78	7	42	7	44
8	38	8	116	8	151
9	69	9	86	9	113
10	78	10	23	10	87
11	29	11	88	11	120
12	47	12	53	12	125
		13	91	13	84
		14	87	14	105
		15	128	15	25
		16	119	16	97
		17	86	17	60
		18	78	18	60
		19	120	19	77

Pg 24	
No.	**Answer**
1	100 + 10 + 10 + 1 = 121
2	100 + 1 + 1 + 1 + 1 + 1 = 105
3	100 + 100 + 100 + 100 + 100 + 10 = 510
4	10 + 10 + 10 + 10 + 1 + 1 = 42
5	100 + 100 + 10 + 10 + 10 + 10 = 240
6	100 + 10 + 1 + 1 + 1 +1 = 114
7	100 + 100 + 100 + 10 + 1 + 1 = 312
8	100 + 10 + 10 + 10 +10 + 1 = 141

Pg 25	
No.	Answer
1	1,000 + 100 + 10 + 1 + 1 = 1,112
2	1,000 + 1,000 + 1,000 + 100 + 1 = 3,101
3	1,000 + 100 + 100 + 10 + 1 + 1 = 1,212
4	1,000 + 1,000 + 1,000 + 1,000 + 100 = 4,100
5	1,000 + 1,000 + 100 + 100 + 10 + 10 = 2,220
6	100 + 10 + 10 + 1 + 1 + 1 = 123
7	1,000 + 1,000 + 100 + 10 + 10 + 1 = 2,121
8	100 + 100 + 100 + 10 + 10 + 1 = 321

Pg 26		Pg 27		Pg 28	
No.	Answer	No.	Answer	No.	Answer
1	1,806	1	1,773	1	2,387
2	892	2	2,782	2	1,190
3	1,330	3	851	3	3,055
4	923	4	1,437	4	2,254
5	1,322	5	1,648	5	1,569
6	831	6	1,286	6	2,266
7	389	7	899	7	1,619
8	1,054	8	1,208	8	2,094
9	1,580	9	2,228	9	1,536
10	204	10	1,511	10	2,321
11	964	11	1,054	11	1,485
12	876	12	1,947	12	1,481
13	1,364	13	1,673	13	1,038
14	648	14	1,395	14	1,833
15	714	15	722	15	1,182
16	1,030				
17	1,046				
18	562				
19	975				

Pg 29

Fill in the blanks to complete each problem.

1. <u>1</u> 2 4
    + 1 9 <u>1</u>
    ———————
      3 1 5

2. 2 <u>3</u> 9
    + <u>6</u> 3 2
    ———————
      8 7 1

3. 3 4 8
    + <u>6</u> 3 <u>1</u>
    ———————
      9 7 9

4. 6 <u>2</u> 3
    + 2 <u>2</u> 2
    ———————
      8 4 5

5. <u>1</u> 3 7
    + 4 <u>4</u> 7
    ———————
      5 8 4

6. 5 8 <u>3</u>
    + <u>3</u> 9 1
    ———————
      9 7 4

7. 3 7 5
    + 1 <u>7</u> 5
    ———————
      5 5 0

8. <u>1</u> 1 5
    + 1 2 <u>2</u>
    ———————
      2 3 7

9. <u>4</u> 2 4
    + 1 2 3
    ———————
      5 4 7

10. 5 <u>2</u> 4
    + <u>2</u> 6 1
    ———————
      7 8 5

11. <u>2</u> 3 4
    + 1 6 <u>2</u>
    ———————
      3 9 6

Pg 30		Pg 31	
No.	Answer	No.	Answer
1	5,501	1	7,641
2	7,061	2	10,626
3	8,636	3	11,044
4	8,023	4	21,672
5	8,711	5	19,295
6	9,482	6	22,701
7	4,121	7	19,214
8	15,195	8	23,256
9	18,911	9	18,628
10	6,526	10	11,171
11	14,723	11	9,686
12	8,041	12	21,667
13	7,905		
14	10,164		
15	4,399		

● Add the numbers going down
● Add the numbers going across,
● Then add your answers together, either across or down, to fill in the the last square

3	4	7
2	3	5
5	7	(12)

1.

1	5	6
5	2	7
6	7	(13)

2.

2	8	10
8	9	17
10	17	(27)

3.

6	3	9
3	6	9
9	9	(18)

4.

2	15	17
15	2	17
17	17	(34)

5.

25	4	29
4	10	14
29	14	(43)

6.

1	8	9
8	40	48
9	48	(57)

Pg 32

● Add the numbers going down
● Add the numbers going across,
● Then add your answers together, either across or down, to fill in the the last square

3	4	7
2	3	5
5	7	(12)

1.

10	3	13
3	10	13
13	13	(26)

2.

5	8	13
8	5	13
13	13	(26)

3.

1	7	8
7	1	8
8	8	(16)

4.

3	6	9
6	12	18
9	18	(27)

5.

70	13	83
13	45	58
83	58	(141)

6.

2	36	38
36	2	38
38	38	(76)

Pg 33

- 11 -

Chapter 3 – Subtraction

Pg 35		Pg 36		Pg 37		Pg 38	
No.	**Answer**	**No.**	**Answer**	**No.**	**Answer**	**No.**	**Answer**
1	13	1	2	1	44	1	28
2	5	2	7	2	45	2	37
3	5	3	7	3	23	3	66
4	36	4	4	4	8	4	42
5	37	5	53	5	23	5	526
6	20	6	61	6	55	6	612
7	22	7	6	7	9	7	523
8	22	8	48	8	8	8	472
9	27	9	68	9	52	9	678
10	14	10	40	10	41	10	378
11	59	11	8	11	33	11	65
12	43	12	60	12	36	12	605
		13	35	13	28	13	341
		14	48	14	61	14	483
		15	17	15	35	15	157
		16	8	16	55	16	77
		17	36	17	2	17	361
		18	31	18	18	18	313
		19	14	19	30	19	87

Pg 39		Pg 40		Pg 41		Pg 42	
No.	Answer	No.	Answer	No.	Answer	No.	Answer
1	380	1	182	1	85	1	105
2	658	2	119	2	32	2	80
3	204	3	299	3	136	3	170
4	261	4	106	4	42	4	30
5	457	5	87	5	81	5	135
6	3	6	156	6	53	6	20
7	204	7	155	7	83	7	119
8	277	8	260	8	73	8	199
9	339	9	77	9	112	9	41
10	769	10	110	10	74	10	86
11	359	11	425	11	20	11	50
12	338	12	55	12	61	12	40
13	551	13	208	13	37	13	60
14	249	14	234	14	160	14	15
15	769	15	23	15	40	15	30
16	555	16	236	16	57	16	30
17	520	17	502	17	92	17	187
18	166	18	592	18	16	18	75
19	794	19	104	19	356	19	180
				20	30	20	161

Pg 43		Pg 44		Pg 45		Pg 46	
No.	Answer	No.	Answer	No.	Answer	No.	Answer
1	194	1	2,071	1	3,366	1	1,889
2	591	2	2,009	2	904	2	4,267
3	122	3	8,920	3	2,459	3	1,044
4	793	4	2,980	4	154	4	2,589
5	377	5	3,331	5	861	5	3,679
6	881	6	4,091	6	1,248	6	19
7	587	7	5,071	7	3,761	7	889
8	314	8	4,334	8	3,626	8	489
9	233	9	2,781	9	5,071	9	1,175
10	195	10	5,565	10	1,925	10	2,689
11	619	11	7,573	11	2,075	11	1,230
12	214	12	1,121	12	111	12	6,495
13	55	13	1,213	13	3,454	13	3,353
14	66	14	1,151	14	320	14	3,984
15	378						
16	46						
17	473						
18	95						
19	66						

Pg 47	
No.	Answer
1	4,690
2	5,844
3	2,045
4	2,571
5	1,784
6	4,222
7	5,406
8	5,897
9	6,122
10	5,009
11	5,329
12	408
13	9,036
14	676

Chapter 4 - Division

Divide the objects equally by the animals for each group.

Objects	Animals	Answer
10 Bananas		5
15 Nuts		3
9 Cheeses		3
14 Bones		7
20 Carrots		5

Pg 51

Divide each group by the numbers in each box and write the answers.

÷ 4 = 2
÷ 2 = 4

÷ 5 = 2
÷ 2 = 5

÷ 3 = 4
÷ 2 = 6

÷ 3 = 5
÷ 5 = 3

÷ 5 = 4
÷ 4 = 5
÷ 2 = 10

÷ 8 = 3
÷ 4 = 6
÷ 2 = 12

Pg 50

Pg 52	
No.	Answer
1	18, 9, 2
2	16, 4, 4
3	125, 5, 25
4	15, 3, 5
5	100, 10, 10
6	72, 9, 8
7	4, 12, 3
8	5, 30, 6
9	6, 42, 7
10	8, 64, 8
11	2, 10, 5
12	3, 21, 7

Pg 53		Pg 54		Pg 55	
No.	Answer	No.	Answer	No.	Answer
1	7	1	24 ÷ 8 = 3, 24 ÷ 6 = 4	1	6
2	7	2	15 ÷ 3 = 5, 15 ÷ 5 = 3	2	5
3	46	3	10 ÷ 2 = 5, 10 ÷ 5 = 2	3	6
4	52	4	50 ÷ 5 = 10, 50 ÷ 10 = 5	4	4
5	28			5	4
6	37			6	9
7	27			7	8
8	33			8	9
9	22			9	8
10	99			10	8
11	59				
12	82				
13	80				
14	90				
15	30				
16	97				
17	46				
18	95				
19	59				
20	65				

Pg 56		Pg 57		Pg 58		Pg 59	
No.	Answer	No.	Answer	No.	Answer	No.	Answer
1	10	1	20	1	8	1	14
2	4	2	4	2	18	2	5
3	5	3	25	3	10	3	7
4	5	4	15	4	6	4	10
5	7	5	6	5	3	5	7
6	1	6	10	6	4	6	9
7	5	7	5	7	2	7	18
8	10	8	25	8	10	8	10
9	3	9	19	9	7	9	5
10	6	10	12	10	5	10	4
		11	22	11	17	11	36
		12	30	12	6	12	6
		13	10	13	13	13	10
		14	42	14	18	14	36
		15	6	15	21	15	5
		16	18	16	40	16	7
						17	100
						18	10
						19	40
						20	15

Pg 60	
No.	Answer
1	30
2	5
3	63
4	29
5	2
6	7
7	48
8	5
9	4
10	3
11	92
12	9
13	10
14	55
15	6
16	8
17	22
18	7
19	14
20	16

Chapter 5 – Fractions

Pg 63

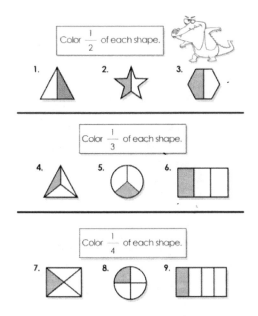

Color $\frac{1}{2}$ of each shape.

1.
2.
3.

Color $\frac{1}{3}$ of each shape.

4.
5.
6.

Color $\frac{1}{4}$ of each shape.

7.
8.
9.

Pg 64

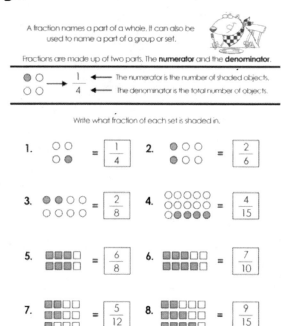

A fraction names a part of a whole. It can also be used to name a part of a group or set.

Fractions are made up of two parts. The **numerator** and the **denominator**.

$\frac{1}{4}$ ← The numerator is the number of shaded objects.
← The denominator is the total number of objects.

Write what fraction of each set is shaded in.

1. $= \dfrac{1}{4}$ 2. $= \dfrac{2}{6}$

3. $= \dfrac{2}{8}$ 4. $= \dfrac{4}{15}$

5. $= \dfrac{6}{8}$ 6. $= \dfrac{7}{10}$

7. $= \dfrac{5}{12}$ 8. $= \dfrac{9}{15}$

Pg 65

A fraction names a part of a whole. It can also be used to name a part of a group or set.

Fractions are made up of two parts. The **numerator** and the **denominator**.

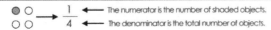

● ○ → $\frac{1}{4}$ ← The numerator is the number of shaded objects.
○ ○ ← The denominator is the total number of objects.

Color each set to match the fraction.

1. $\frac{1}{4}$ = ○ ○ / ○ ●

2. $\frac{2}{8}$ = ● ● ○ / ○ ○ ○

3. $\frac{1}{8}$ = ● ○ ○ ○ / ○ ○ ○ ○

4. $\frac{7}{15}$ = ○○○○○ / ○○●●● / ●●●●○

5. $\frac{3}{8}$ = □□□□ / ■■□□

6. $\frac{6}{10}$ = □□□□■ / ■■■■■

7. $\frac{1}{2}$ = ■■■■ / ■■□□ / □□□□

8. $\frac{5}{15}$ = ■■■■■ / □□□□□ / □□□□□

Pg 66

Draw a line to match the fractions.

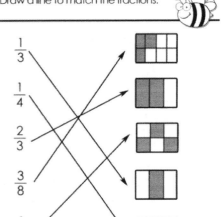

$\frac{1}{3}$

$\frac{1}{4}$

$\frac{2}{3}$

$\frac{3}{8}$

$\frac{1}{2}$

Pg 67

Write the fraction shown in each shape.
Write the shaded amount as the top number.

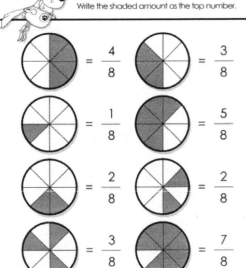

= $\frac{4}{8}$ = $\frac{3}{8}$

= $\frac{1}{8}$ = $\frac{5}{8}$

= $\frac{2}{8}$ = $\frac{2}{8}$

= $\frac{3}{8}$ = $\frac{7}{8}$

Pg 68

Write the fraction shown in each shape.
Write the shaded amount as the top number.

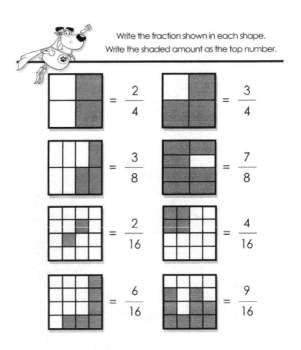

= $\frac{2}{4}$ = $\frac{3}{4}$

= $\frac{3}{8}$ = $\frac{7}{8}$

= $\frac{2}{16}$ = $\frac{4}{16}$

= $\frac{6}{16}$ = $\frac{9}{16}$

- 20 -

Pg 69

Color each shape to match the fraction.

$\frac{1}{4}$ = $\frac{1}{2}$ =

$\frac{3}{8}$ = $\frac{5}{8}$ =

$\frac{5}{16}$ = $\frac{9}{16}$ =

$\frac{2}{16}$ = $\frac{7}{16}$ =

Pg 70

The whole number **1** can be shown by many fractions.
When the numerator and denominator match, the fraction equals **1**.

$\frac{6}{6}$ = 1	$\frac{8}{8}$ = 1	$\frac{3}{3}$ = 1

Another way to show a whole number as a fraction is to
use **1** for the denominator.

$2 = \frac{2}{1}$	$4 = \frac{4}{1}$	$9 = \frac{9}{1}$

Complete the fractions.

1. $1 = \frac{5}{5}$ 2. $1 = \frac{8}{8}$ 3. $1 = \frac{3}{3}$

4. $1 = \frac{14}{14}$ 5. $1 = \frac{6}{6}$ 6. $1 = \frac{10}{10}$

Write the fraction that equals the whole number.

1. $5 = \frac{5}{1}$ 2. $14 = \frac{14}{1}$ 3. $9 = \frac{9}{1}$

4. $72 = \frac{72}{1}$ 5. $3 = \frac{3}{1}$ 6. $18 = \frac{18}{1}$

Pg 71

Color the correct number of objects for each fraction.

1. $\dfrac{5}{6}$

2. $\dfrac{1}{3}$

3. $\dfrac{7}{10}$

4. $\dfrac{1}{2}$

5. $\dfrac{1}{3}$

6. $\dfrac{3}{10}$

7. $\dfrac{1}{4}$

8. $\dfrac{2}{3}$

Pg 72

Just because two fractions are the same, that does not mean they are the same amount.

Half of each circle is shaded. Notice that shape **A** is larger than **B**. They each show a different amount.

Here are two different ways to write this:

$\dfrac{1}{2}$ of **A** is greater than $\dfrac{1}{2}$ of **B**   OR $\dfrac{1}{2}$ **A** $\boxed{>}$ $\dfrac{1}{2}$ **B**

Write out the fractions, then compare the fractions.

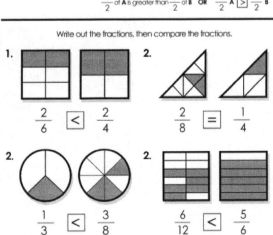

1. $\dfrac{2}{6}$ $\boxed{<}$ $\dfrac{2}{4}$

2. $\dfrac{2}{8}$ $\boxed{=}$ $\dfrac{1}{4}$

2. $\dfrac{1}{3}$ $\boxed{<}$ $\dfrac{3}{8}$

2. $\dfrac{6}{12}$ $\boxed{<}$ $\dfrac{5}{6}$

Pg 73

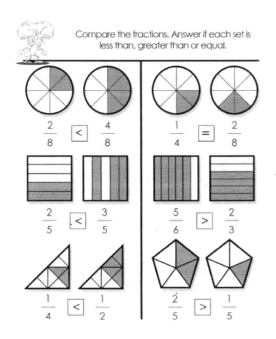

Compare the fractions. Answer if each set is less than, greater than or equal.

$\frac{2}{8}$ [<] $\frac{4}{8}$ $\frac{1}{4}$ [=] $\frac{2}{8}$

$\frac{2}{5}$ [<] $\frac{3}{5}$ $\frac{5}{6}$ [>] $\frac{2}{3}$

$\frac{1}{4}$ [<] $\frac{1}{2}$ $\frac{2}{5}$ [>] $\frac{1}{5}$

Pg 74

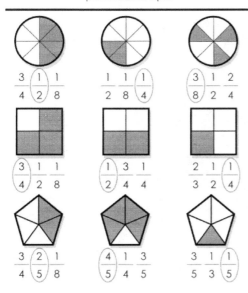

Circle the fraction that matches the shaded parts in each shape.

$\frac{3}{4}$ $\left(\frac{1}{2}\right)$ $\frac{1}{8}$ $\frac{1}{2}$ $\frac{1}{8}$ $\left(\frac{1}{4}\right)$ $\left(\frac{3}{8}\right)$ $\frac{1}{2}$ $\frac{2}{4}$

$\left(\frac{3}{4}\right)$ $\frac{1}{2}$ $\frac{1}{8}$ $\left(\frac{1}{2}\right)$ $\frac{3}{4}$ $\frac{1}{4}$ $\frac{2}{3}$ $\frac{1}{2}$ $\left(\frac{1}{4}\right)$

$\frac{3}{4}$ $\left(\frac{2}{5}\right)$ $\frac{1}{8}$ $\left(\frac{4}{5}\right)$ $\frac{1}{4}$ $\frac{3}{5}$ $\frac{3}{5}$ $\frac{1}{3}$ $\left(\frac{1}{5}\right)$

Chapter 6 – Multiplication

Pg 76

Multiplication is the way we find the sum of the same number a certain amount of times.

$4 \times 2 = 8$
$2 + 2 + 2 + 2 = 8$
□□ □□ □□ □□

$2 \times 5 = 10$
$5 + 5 = 10$
□□ □□
□□ □□
□ □

Break each group down by writing them out,
then adding them together.

1. $3 \times 2 = 6$
$\underline{2} + \underline{2} + \underline{2} = \underline{6}$

2. $3 \times 4 = 12$
$\underline{4} + \underline{4} + \underline{4} = \underline{12}$

3. $4 \times 4 = 16$
$\underline{4} + \underline{4} + \underline{4} + \underline{4} = \underline{16}$

4. $4 \times 5 = 20$
$\underline{5} + \underline{5} + \underline{5} + \underline{5} = \underline{20}$

5. $3 \times 8 = 24$
$\underline{8} + \underline{8} + \underline{8} = \underline{24}$

6. $4 \times 10 = 40$
$\underline{10} + \underline{10} + \underline{10} + \underline{10} = \underline{40}$

5. $2 \times 6 = 12$
$\underline{6} + \underline{6} = \underline{12}$

6. $3 \times 6 = 18$
$\underline{6} + \underline{6} + \underline{6} = \underline{18}$

Pg 77			
No.	Answer	No.	Answer
1	0	12	4
2	4	13	6
3	1	14	5
4	9	15	3
5	9	16	0
6	6	17	2
7	2	18	7
8	8	19	8
9	6	20	7
10	0	21	0
11	3		

Pg 78		Pg 79		Pg 80		Pg 81	
No.	Answer	No.	Answer	No.	Answer	No.	Answer
1	18	1	6	1	3	1	12
2	8	2	0	2	0	2	10
3	16	3	4	3	20	3	35
4	7	4	14	4	12	4	18
5	18	5	24	5	4	5	0
6	10	6	12	6	16	6	5
7	7	7	18	7	0	7	18
8	4	8	24	8	28	8	40
9	6	9	0	9	8	9	0
10	6	10	16	10	2	10	16
11	18	11	27	11	36	11	30
12	8	12	21	12	20	12	25
13	14	13	0	13	32	13	4
14	10	14	9	14	4	14	45
15	0	15	2	15	0	15	18
16	12	16	7	16	24	16	16
17	16	17	0	17	18	17	0
18	0	18	15	18	27	18	15
19	4	19	9	19	12	19	9
20	2	20	15	20	12	20	10
21	8	21	18	21	27	21	18

Pg 82		Pg 83		Pg 84		Pg 85	
No.	Answer	No.	Answer	No.	Answer	No.	Answer
1	0	1	12	1	56	1	9
2	54	2	0	2	16	2	36
3	15	3	20	3	8	3	56
4	8	4	3	4	12	4	81
5	12	5	42	5	0	5	21
6	6	6	14	6	35	6	40
7	14	7	9	7	72	7	9
8	18	8	21	8	15	8	3
9	36	9	63	9	24	9	24
10	4	10	24	10	0	10	2
11	30	11	28	11	16	11	54
12	24	12	30	12	25	12	16
13	0	13	4	13	16	13	35
14	25	14	35	14	56	14	45
15	27	15	14	15	40	15	36
16	12	16	42	16	72	16	36
17	30	17	7	17	64	17	0
18	15	18	49	18	32	18	18
19	48	19	56	19	32	19	21
20	42	20	7	20	10	20	10
21	0	21	42	21	24	21	27

Pg 86		Pg 87		Pg 88		Pg 89	
No.	Answer	No.	Answer	No.	Answer	No.	Answer
1	3	1	30	1	400	1	48
2	4	2	20	2	200	2	219
3	5	3	50	3	500	3	120
4	9	4	60	4	600	4	128
5	6	5	10	5	100	5	48
6	2	6	50	6	400	6	63
7	10	7	40	7	800	7	75
8	8	8	80	8	900	8	108
9	6	9	70	9	0	9	49
10	7	10	0	10	700	10	76
		11	90	11	300		
		12	20	12	700		
		13	40	13	400		
		14	30	14	300		
		15	90	15	900		

Chapter 7 – Graphing

Pg 91

Draw a line on the graph to answer each question.

1. Tom is six years old.
2. Laney is seven years old.
3. Jane is two years old.
4. Stan is three years old.
5. Sally is one year old.
6. Mark is ten years old.
7. Mike is four years old.
8. Anne is eight years old.
9. Elle is five years old.
10. Donnie is nine years old.

Pg 92

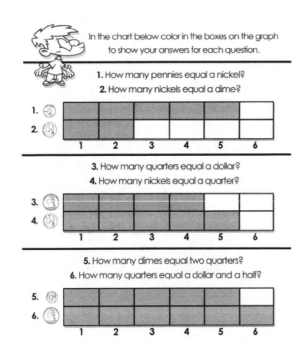

In the chart below color in the boxes on the graph to show your answers for each question.

1. How many pennies equal a nickel?
2. How many nickels equal a dime?

3. How many quarters equal a dollar?
4. How many nickels equal a quarter?

5. How many dimes equal two quarters?
6. How many quarters equal a dollar and a half?

- 28 -

Pg 93

Use the graph to answer the questions.

1. What was the coldest month? __December__

2. What was the hottest month? __July__

3. What was the temperature in March? __35 degrees__

4. About how many degrees was the difference between the coldest and hottest months? __40-45 degrees__

5. What was the temperature in November? __30 degrees__

6. Did it become hotter or colder from April to May? __hotter__

7. Did the temperature change from September to October? __no__

8. Which month was colder, January or December? __December__

Pg 95	
No.	**Answer**
1	pancakes
2	ham
3	bacon
4	ham
5	bacon
6	pancakes
7	eggs

Pg 96

Color in a square for each object you see in the picture below.

Pg 97		Pg 98	
No.	**Answer**	**No.**	**Answer**
1	3	1	$50
2	5	2	13 miles
3	2	3	32 pieces of candy
4	4	4	97 cupcakes
5	5		
6	1		
7	6		

Pg 99

Locate the points on the grid and draw the shapes for each question.

1. A, 4 - ◯

2. C, 1 - ⬡

3. K, 6 - △

4. H, 3 - ♡

5. F, 6 - ☆

6. L, 1 - ⬯

Chapter 8 - Money & Time

Pg 103		Pg 104		Pg 105		Pg 106	
No.	Answer	No.	Answer	No.	Answer	No.	Answer
1	76¢	1	$1.41	1	25¢	1	$3.95
2	72¢	2	$3.12	2	23¢	2	$2.39
3	$1.55	3	$7.61	3	36¢	3	$1.68
4	$1.86	4	$30.18	4	52¢	4	$4.39
5	93¢	5	$25.87	5	$3.93	5	$3.91
6	$1.81	6	$35.33	6	$3.64	6	$6.79
7	$1.36			7	$4.36	7	$9.19
8	$1.09					8	$13.20
9	$1.45						

Pg 107	
No.	Answer
1	thirty-eight dollars and fifty-nine cents
2	one-hundred dollars and thirty-two cents
3	two-hundred seventy-eight dollars and twelve cents
4	three-hundred fifteen dollars and eight cents
5	nine-hundred fifteen dollars and eighty-three cents
6	eighteen dollars and thirty-three cents
7	two-hundred twenty-nine dollars and twenty-nine cents
8	seven-hundred fifty-six dollars and ten cents
9	six-hundred eighteen dollars and twenty-four cents
10	nine-hundred ninety-nine dollars and seventy-two cents

Pg 109

Draw a line from each clock on the left to match the clock on the right.

8:35

3:25

1:25

10:05

Pg 110		Pg 111	
No.	Answer	No.	Answer
1	AM	1	6 hours 45 minutes
2	PM	2	9 hours 26 minutes
3	AM	3	5 hours 12 minutes
4	PM	4	15 hours 52 minutes
5	PM	5	3 hours 45 minutes
6	AM	6	1 hour 54 minutes
7	PM	7	58 minutes
8	PM	8	3 hours 48 minutes
9	AM		
10	PM		

Pg 112

Write the correct times in the clocks on the right.

9:15	10:30
What time will it be in 3 hours and 15 minutes?	What time will it be in 2 hours and 30 minutes?
12:15	4:45
What time will it be in 1 hour and 45 minutes?	What time will it be in 2 hours and 15 minutes?
5:15	8:45
What time will it be in 4 hours and 45 minutes?	What time will it be in 3 hours and 30 minutes?
8:45	9:45
What time will it be in 5 hours and 45 minutes?	What time will it be in 1 hour and 15 minutes?

Pg 113

Draw the hands on the clock to show the proper times.

What time will it be in 2 hours and 20 minutes?	What time will it be in 1 hour and 35 minutes?
What time will it be in 3 hours and 5 minutes?	What time will it be in 6 hours and 10 minutes?
What time will it be in 3 hours and 25 minutes?	What time will it be in 3 hours and 15 minutes?
What time will it be in 5 hours and 35 minutes?	What time will it be in 3 hours and 15 minutes?

- 34 -

Chapter 9 - Geometry & Measurements

Pg 116

How many smaller shapes can you find in each larger shape? Write your answer.

Pg 117

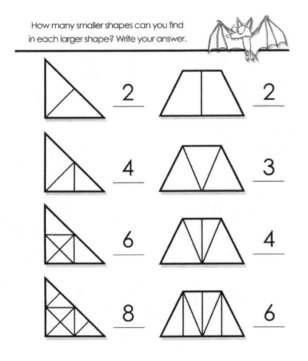

How many smaller shapes can you find in each larger shape? Write your answer.

Pg 118

Write inside each shape how many sides it has.
Then answer each question.

1. ⑤ has how many more sides than 4 ? 1

2. ⑧ has how many more sides than △3 ? 5

3. How many total sides do you get when you add
   ⟋4⟍ with a ⟨6⟩ ? 10

4. ⑩ has how many more sides than ⑦ ? 3

5. How many total sides do you get when you add
   ⑧ with a △3 ? 11

Pg 119	
No.	**Answer**
1	3
2	4
3	6
4	7
5	4
6	7
7	7
8	6

Pg 120

Area is the amount of space inside a shape.

Use the grid to draw the shapes for each question.

1. Draw 3 shapes with an area of 2 units each.
2. Draw 2 shapes with an area of 7 units each.
3. Draw 4 shapes with an area of 5 units each.
4. Draw 3 shapes with an area of 9 units each.
5. Draw 2 shapes with an area of 11 units each.

Pg 121		Pg 122	
No.	Answer	No.	Answer
1	4 + 6 + 4 +6 = 20 in	1	8
2	7 + 7 + 7 = 21ft	2	10
3	8 + 20 + 20 + 26 = 74in	3	9
4	12 + 8 + 12 + 8 = 40ft	4	12
5	6 + 6 + 9 +6 + 9 = 36in	5	10
6	3 + 3 + 3 + 3 + 3 + 3 = 18ft	6	12
		7	14
		8	14

Pg 123   Answers can vary

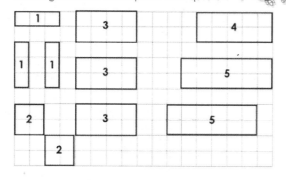

Perimeter is the distance around a two-dimensional shape.

Use the grid to draw the shapes for each question.

1. Draw 3 shapes with a perimeter of 8 units each.

2. Draw 2 shapes with a perimeter of 20 units each.

3. Draw 3 shapes with a perimeter of 12 units each.

4. Draw 1 shapes with a perimeter of 14 units each.

5. Draw 2 shapes with a perimeter of 16 units each.

Pg 124			
No.	**Answer**	**No.**	**Answer**
1	line segment	1	XY or DF
2	point	2	line segment
3	line	3	any point on the illustration
4	line segment	4	line
		5	E

Pg 125		Pg 126		Pg 127		Pg 128	
No.	Answer	No.	Answer	No.	Answer	No.	Answer
1	obtuse	1	Ounces	1	yards	1	cup
2	acute	2	Pounds	2	feet	2	gallon
3	right	3	Ounces	3	miles	3	pint
4	obtuse	4	Pounds	4	feet	4	quart
		5	Pounds	5	feet	5	pint
		6	Ounces	6	miles	6	gallon
				7	feet		
				8	yards		
				9	miles		
				10	foot		

Practice Test #1 Answers

Answers and Explanations

TEKS Standard §111.5(b)(1)(D)

1. B: The number, 860,002 has an 8 in the hundred-thousands place, a 6 in the ten-thousands place, a 0 in the thousands place, a 0 in the hundreds place, a 0 in the tens place, and a 2 in the ones place. The 860 written in front of the comma represents, "Eight hundred sixty thousand." The 2 in the ones place represents, "Two." Therefore, the number is read, "Eight hundred sixty thousand, two."

TEKS Standard §111.5(b)(2)(D)

2. D: The annual expenses for Years 2009, 2007, 2008, 2011, and 2010 are $1,046, $1,224, $1,319, $1,342, and $1,529, respectively. These amounts are listed in order from lowest to highest. Since all of the numbers have a 1 in the thousands place, the numerals in the hundreds place must be compared. For the amounts of $1,319 and $1,342, the numerals in the tens place must be compared. No other choice shows the years listed in increasing order of expense.

TEKS Standard §111.5(b)(4)(C)

3. C: There are 2 dollar bills, which represent 2 dollars. There are also 2 quarters, 2 nickels, 1 dime, and 4 pennies. Two quarters are worth $0.50 since each is worth $0.25 ($2 \times 0.25 = 0.50$) , 2 nickels are worth $0.10 since each is worth $0.05 ($2 \times 0.05 = 0.10$) , 1 dime is worth $0.10, and 4 pennies are worth $0.04 since each is worth $0.01. The sum of the coins can be found by writing: $0.50 + $0.10 + $0.10 + $0.04, which equals $0.74. The sum of the two dollar bills and the coins can be written as: $2.00 + $0.74. Thus, he paid $2.74.

TEKS Standard §111.5(b)(3)(A)

4. B: If 1/3 of the balls Wyatt received were basketballs that means the remaining balls he received must have been soccer balls. Since the fraction used is 1/3, look at it as if he received 3 balls. One ball was a basketball and the remaining balls had to be soccer balls. This is now a simple subtraction problem. 3 – 1 = 2 soccer balls.

TEKS Standard §111.5(b)(2)(D)

5. D: The numbers: 608, 458, 452, 381, 321, and 294 are written in order from greatest to least. An examination of the numerals in the hundreds place reveals that 608 is the greatest and 294 is the least. The numbers, 458 and 452, are greater than the numbers, 381 and 321, based on the value of the digits in the hundreds place. An examination of the numerals in the ones place, since both the digits in the hundreds and the tens places are the same, allows you to compare 458 and 452, which shows 458 to be the larger number. An examination of the numerals in the tens place allows you to compare 381 and 321, since the digits in the hundreds place are the same, which shows 381 to be the larger number. None of the other choices show the numbers in descending order.

TEKS Standard §111.5(b)(3)(A)

6. C: Choice C shows 2 triangles and 4 hexagons, which is a total of 6 shapes. The fraction 2 out of 6, or $\frac{2}{6}$, also represents 1 out of 3, or $\frac{1}{3}$. None of the other choices represent this fraction: Choice A shows $\frac{3}{6}$, which equals $\frac{1}{2}$. Choice B shows $\frac{1}{4}$. Choice D shows $\frac{1}{6}$.

TEKS Standard §111.5(b)(4)(E)

7. C: The diagram shows 32 counters divided into 4 groups, with 8 counters in each group. Therefore, the total number of counters, 32, is divided by 4, giving a quotient of 8, which is written as: 32 ÷ 4 = 8.

TEKS Standard §111.5(b)(4)(G)

8. This is a simple multiplication problem which involves carrying the excess (greater than a single digit) to the next column. Start with the 8 and multiply each digit above: 8 x 6 = 48. Write down the 8 and place the 4 on top of the 9. Multiply 8 x 9 to get 72. Add in the 4 to get 76. Write down the number 76 and the product is 768.

TEKS Standard §111.5(b)(4)(A)

9. D: The total number of feet he ascended can be determined by adding 482 feet and 362 feet. The sum of 482 and 362 is 844. Thus, he ascended 844 feet in all.

TEKS Standard §111.5(b)(4)(B)

10. C: The item priced at $4.58 can be rounded to $5. The item priced at $6.22 can be rounded to $6. The item priced at $8.94 can be rounded to $9. The sum of 5, 6 and 9 is 20. Thus, the best estimate is $20.

TEKS Standard §111.5(b)(3)(A)

11. B: Choice B shows 4 shaded sections out of 6 total sections. The fraction, $\frac{4}{6}$, is the same as the fraction, $\frac{2}{3}$. Two shaded sections represent one-third of the total. Thus, four shaded sections represent two-thirds of the total. Each of the pictures has 6 total sections, so the other choices can be written as fractions with a 6 in the denominator. Choice A shows $\frac{3}{6}$, which equals $\frac{1}{2}$. Choice C shows . Choice D shows $\frac{2}{6}$, which equals $\frac{1}{3}$. So, only Choice B shows the correct picture.

TEKS Standard §111.5(b)(4)(K)

12. D: A possible first step would be to divide the number of tiles glued each day by the number of hours it took to glue the tiles. The two quotients would then represent approximately how many tiles glued per hour, and could then be compared.

TEKS Standard §111.5(b)(4)(B) and (4)(K)

13. Begin with the tokens given to each guest, which was 12. But the problem states that every game takes two tokens, so each guest can play only 6 games, not 12. Multiply this by the number of guests, 12, to equal 72 games. Round this number to the nearest tens to get 70.

TEKS Standard §111.5(b)(5)

14. C: Each number is 8 more than the previous number, which means that the next number can be found by adding 8 to the previous number. Thus, the fifth number is 353, the sixth number is 361, the seventh number is 369, and the eighth number is 377.

TEKS Standard §111.5(b)(4)(C)

15. C: Convert the coins to cents and apply addition. Each nickel is worth 5 cents, so 3 nickels equals 15 cents. Each dime is worth 10 cents, so 4 dimes equals 40 cents. Each penny is worth 1 cent, so 2 pennies equals 2 cents. A quarter is worth 25 cents, so 2 quarters equals 50 cents.. 15 + 40 + 2 + 50 = 107 cents. Since there are 100 cents in a dollar, this becomes 1 dollar with 7 cents remaining or $1.07

TEKS Standard §111.5(b)(5)

16. C: Each figure has 3 more squares than the previous figure, so adding 3 to the number of squares in the previous figure yields the number of squares in the next figure. Thus, he will use 14 squares for Figure 5, 17 squares for Figure 6, 20 squares for Figure7, 23 squares for Figure 8, and 26 squares for Figure 9.

TEKS Standard §111.5(b)(5)(B)

17. C: In order to find the amount donated the following year, you multiply the amount donated the previous year by 3. Thus, the amount donated the second year was $6 ($2 × 3). The amount donated the third year was $18 ($6 × 3). The amount donated the fourth year was $54 ($18 × 3). The amount donated the fifth year was $162 ($54 × 3).

TEKS Standard §111.5(b)(5)(D) and (4)(A)

18. The correct answer is 4. 4 X 3 = 12; 16 - 4 =12, and 8 + 4 = 12.

TEKS Standard §111.5(b)(4)(K)

19. D: Each spider has 8 legs. In order to find the number of legs present with 3 spiders, you multiply 3 by 8, which is 24. Thus, 3 spiders have 24 legs in all. Choice D is the only table that shows each number of spiders, multiplied by 8, to yield the correct product representing the total number of legs.

TEKS Standard §111.5(b)(4)(K)

20. C: Each candy jar has 14 pieces of candy. This can be determined by dividing the number of pieces of candy by the number of candy jars: $28 \div 2 = 14, 56 \div 4 = 14, 70 \div 5 = 14, 126 \div 9 = 14$. Since the data in the table shows that there are 14 pieces of candy in each jar, multiplying $13 \times 14 = 182$ finds the total number of pieces of candy that are in 13 candy jars.

TEKS Standard §111.5(b)(4)(K)

21. D: If she drinks 8 glasses of water each day, the number of glasses of water she drinks in 12 days can be determined by multiplying 8 by 12. This product is 96; thus she drinks 96 glasses of water in a 12-day time span. The relationship between the number of glasses of water she drinks per day and the total number of glasses of water she drinks in 12 days can be represented by an appropriate multiplication or division number sentence within the following fact family: $8 \times 12 = 96, 96 \div 8 = 12, 12 \times 8 = 96, 96 \div 12 = 8$. Subtracting 8 from 12 will not reveal the number of glasses she drinks in a 12-day time span. The number sentence: $12 - 8 = ?$, is not in this fact family.

TEKS Standard §111.5 (b)(5)

22. C: If each rectangle has a length that is 5 cm more than that of the previous rectangle, the lengths of the 3rd rectangle through the 11th rectangle can be found by adding 5 cm to the length of the second triangle and continuing for each next rectangle. So, the lengths of the rectangles will be as follows: 16 cm, 21 cm, 26 cm, 31 cm, 36 cm, 41 cm, 46 cm, 51 cm, and 56 cm.

TEKS Standard §111.5(b)(5)

23. D: The pattern is subtracting one less number each time:

$$132 - 9 = 123$$
$$123 - 8 = 115$$
$$115 - 7 = 108$$
$$108 - 6 = 102$$

The next number to be subtracted is 5, so $102 - 5 = 97$

TEKS Standard §111.5(b)(6)

24. D: Choices A, B, and C are all the same right triangle just flipped around. Answer choice D is a different triangle and therefore not congruent.

TEKS Standard §111.5(b)(3)

25. D: 12 ¼ is represented by the first tick mark to the right of the 12. 12 ½ is the second tick mark and 12 ¾ is the third tick mark, or the tick mark before the 13. Only 12 ¾ appears to the right of point M on the number line, making it greater.

TEKS Standard §111.5(b)(6)(A)

26. D: An edge is the intersection of two faces. A triangular pyramid (Choice A) has 6 edges, while a triangular prism (Choice B) has 9 edges, a square pyramid (Choice C) has 8 edges, and a cube (Choice D) has 12 edges. The cube is the only figure with more than 9 edges.

TEKS Standard §111.5(b)(6)(A)

27. C: A vertex is a point where two or more edges meet. A triangle has 3 vertices. Two times that would be 6 vertices. The figure shown for Choice C is a triangular prism, which is the only figure that has 6 vertices. A triangular pyramid (Choice A) has 4 vertices, a cube (Choice B) has 8 vertices, and a square pyramid (Choice D) has 5 vertices.

TEKS Standard §111.5(b)(6)(A)

28. C: A cube (Choice C) has 6 faces, while a square pyramid and triangular prism (Choices A and B) each have 5 faces, and a triangular pyramid (Choice D) has 4 faces. So, a cube has the most faces out of these choices.

TEKS Standard §111.5(b)(6)

29. D: The trapezoid shown for Choice D is congruent to the given shape, provided. Basically, the shapes must be the same size to be congruent, but can be flipped or rotated in any way.

TEKS Standard §111.5(b)(6)(A)

30. B: The figure shown is an isosceles trapezoid, and it has 1 line of symmetry, which is a vertical line that passes through the midpoint of each base.

TEKS Standard §111.5(b)(3)(A)

31. B: Each increment represents one-half. This can be determined by counting that there are 3 marks, or 4 spaces, that lie between the difference of two wholes, as in between 10 and 12. Thus, one increment past 10, where Point P is located, represents $10\frac{1}{2}$.

TEKS Standard §111.5(b)(6)(A)

32. B: An octagon has 8 lines of symmetry, and 3 lines of symmetry is 5 fewer than 8 lines of symmetry. An equilateral triangle (Choice B) has 3 lines of symmetry, while a square (Choice A) has 4 lines of symmetry, a pentagon (Choice C) has 5 lines of symmetry, and an isosceles trapezoid (Choice D) has 1 line of symmetry. Thus, an equilateral triangle is the only shape shown that has 5 fewer lines of symmetry than an octagon.

TEKS Standard §111.5(b)(7)(B)

33. B: The distance around the triangle, or the perimeter, is equal to the sum of 3 cm, 5 cm, and 4 cm. Thus, the perimeter is 12 cm.

TEKS Standard §111.5(b)(7)(B)

34. D: The perimeter of the trapezoid is the distance around all of the sides, and is equal to the sum of 3 in, 8 in, 8 in, and 14 in. Thus, the perimeter is 33 in.

TEKS Standard §111.5(b)(6)
35. A: The distance from the center of the circle, marked C, to a point on the circle, is also known as the radius, and it is approximately 2 cm. The distance can be estimated by marking off estimated units of length for a centimeter. Such markings approximate 2 centimeters.

TEKS Standard §111.5(b)(7)
36. B: The crayon measures almost exactly 3 inches.

TEKS Standard §111.5(b)(6)
37. C: The trapezoid has 8 square units, plus 4 one-half square units, which equals 2 more square units. The sum of 8 square units and 2 square units is 10 square units.

TEKS Standard §111.5(b)(7)
38. B: The thermometer shows the temperature to be very close to 80 degrees Fahrenheit. It also shows the temperature in Celsius: about 25 degrees.

TEKS Standard §111.5(b)(7)
39. C: The short hand, or hour hand, is between 6 o'clock and 7 o'clock, revealing that Karen went to the library after 6 o'clock. The long hand, or minute hand, is pointed at the 2. Since the 2 on the clock represents 10 minutes after the hour (since each number shown on the clock represents 5 minutes and $2 \times 5 = 10$), the clock shows that Karen went to the library at 6:10.

TEKS Standard §111.5(b)(7)

40. A: Five o'clock shown on a digital clock would be shown as a 5 followed by two zeroes, indicating no minutes.

TEKS Standard §111.5(b)(8)

41. B: Since a die has one of each number, from 1 to 6, she is equally likely to roll any of the six numbers. The possibility of rolling one of these numbers is no more or less than the possibility of rolling another of these numbers. Thus, she is equally likely to roll a 3 or a 6.

TEKS Standard §111.5(b)(8)

42. D: The more fish there is of a certain color the more likely it is that the color of fish is scooped. With more orange fish than striped fish in the bowl, he is more likely to scoop an orange fish than a striped one. There are equal amounts of striped and blue fish, so one is not more likely than the other. There are more orange fish than blue fish, so he is more likely to scoop an orange fish than a blue one.. Finally, the number of striped and blue fish is the same – so they are equally likely to be scooped compared to each other. Thus, Choice D is the only true statement.

TEKS Standard §111.5(b)(8)

43. C: A die has numbers 1 – 6, so rolling a number less than 8 is a certain occurrence. It will always happen. Choice A is incorrect because rolling a 7 would be impossible. Choices B and D are also incorrect because rolling either an even or odd number, since the die has both, would not be certain.

TEKS Standard §111.5(b)(8)(B)

44. D: Texas has the most zoos because it has 15 zoos, while the other states each have 7 zoos, 4 zoos, and 11 zoos. Also, it can be seen from the graph that the bar representing Texas is much higher than the bars for the other states.

TEKS Standard §111.5(b)(8)(B)

45. C: Baseball received 6 votes and basketball received only 2 votes. The difference is 6 – 2 = 4 fewer votes.

TEKS Standard §111.5(b)(8)

46. A: Since each tree represents 2 lawns, the pictograph shows that the number of lawns finished by Company A is equal to 6 × 2, or 12 lawns, the number of lawns finished by Company B is equal to 9 × 2, or 18 lawns, the number of lawns finished by Company C is equal to 3 × 2, or 6 lawns, and the number of lawns finished by Company D is equal to 8 × 2, or 16 lawns. This is the only pictograph that represents the correct number of lawns.

Practice Test #2 Answers

Answers and Explanations

TEKS Standard §111.5(b)(1)(D)

1. B: The number shown for Choice B correctly shows a 2 in the hundreds place, and a 4 in the ones place.

TEKS Standard §111.5(b)(2)(D)

2. D: All numbers for Choice D have a 5 in the hundreds place, indicating that the next digit, in the tens place, must be used to make comparisons. Each digit in the tens place is different, so an examination of the ones place is not needed. The list of increasing tens place digits for Choice D are 2, 3, 4, 7, and 8, indicating a correct ordering of the numbers from least to greatest. None of the other choices show strictly increasing numbers.

TEKS Standard §111.5(b)(5)(A)

3. C: The term subtracted from means to "take away" and place a minus sign in the equation. Since 5 is being subtracted from 25, write the number 25 first followed by a minus sign and then the number 5. The problem states that this subtraction equals 5, so simply attach this to the end.

TEKS Standard §111.5(b)(3)(A)

4. D: Choice D shows 1 crayon and 3 pencils, indicating that 1 out of 4 of Camille's writing tools were crayons. The other choices are out of either a total of 7 writing tools or 5 writing tools, which cannot be used in a ratio that represents 1 out of 4.

TEKS Standard §111.5(b)(4)(A)

5. D: In order to find out the total number of hot dogs she sold in the two months, the amount sold in each month should be added. The sum of 128 and 117 is 245. Thus, she sold 245 hot dogs during the two months.

TEKS Standard §111.5(b)(4)(C)

6. D: Two dollar bills are worth $2.00. A quarter is worth $0.25, 4 dimes are worth $0.40 since they are worth $0.10 each ($4 \times 0.10 = 0.40$), 3 nickels are worth $0.15 since they are worth $0.05 each ($3 \times 0.05 = 0.15$), and 2 pennies are worth $0.02 since each is worth $0.01. The sum of the coins is: $0.25 + $0.40 + $0.15 + $0.02, which equals $0.82. The sum of the two dollar bills and the coins can be written as: $2.00 + $0.82, which equals $2.82.

TEKS Standard §111.5(b)(4)(E)

7. D: The diagram shows 24 counters total, divided into 3 groups, with 8 counters in each group. Therefore, the total number of counters, 24, is divided by 3. This gives a quotient of 8, which is written as: $24 \div 3 = 8$.

TEKS Standard §111.5(b)(4)(G)

8. This is a simple multiplication problem which involves carrying the excess (greater than a single digit) to the next column. Start with the 9 and multiply each digit above: 9 x 8 = 72. Write down the 2 and place the 7 on top of the 7. Multiply 9 x 7 to get 63. Add in the 7 to get 70. Write down the number 70 and the product is 702.

TEKS Standard §111.5(b)(4)(G)

9. B: The number of customers who entered the store can be rounded to 90. That number can be multiplied by 6, since each customer receives 6 coupons. The product of 90×6 is 540.

TEKS Standard §111.5(b)(1)(B) and (4)(A) and (4)(K)

10. A: Since a chicken has 2 feet and a horse has 4 feet, you may multiply the number of chickens found on each farm by 2, and then multiply the number of horses found on each farm by 4. After finding the total number of chicken feet and horse feet on each farm, you can then add the two amounts to find the total number of animal feet on each farm. You can then compare the two values to determine the one that is larger.

TEKS Standard §111.5(b)(3)(A)

11. B: Each model shows a whole, split into 7 sections. This makes the denominator equal to 7 for the fraction representing the shaded section for each. Since the fractions all have the same number on the bottom, the number of shaded sections can be compared. For a fraction to be more than $\frac{4}{7}$, more than 4 parts must be shaded. The model shown for Choice B shows the fraction $\frac{6}{7}$, because 6 out of 7 sections are shaded, showing a fraction that is more than 4 out of 7. The other choices all show either 4 parts or less than 4 parts shaded.

TEKS Standard §111.5(b)(2)(D)

12. B: The sequence of the number of miles walked in order from greatest to least is: 963 (Year 4), 691 (Year 1), 567 (Year 2), 221 (Year 5), 144 (Year 3). The number of miles walked can also be compared by examining only the digits in the hundreds place since they are all different. 9 is greater than 6 which is greater than 5 and so on. The only choice that shows the years for the number of miles walked in descending order is B.

TEKS Standard §111.5(b)(4)(A) and (4)(B)

13. D: 23 + 12 + 34 = 69. Since the 9 in the ones digit is greater than or equal to five, the number is rounded up to 70.

TEKS Standard §111.5(b)(4)(C)

14. C: Convert the coins to cents and apply addition. Each nickel is worth 5 cents, so 2 nickels equals 10 cents. Each dime is worth 10 cents, so 2 dimes equals 20 cents. Each penny is worth 1 cent, so 4 pennies equals 4 cents. A quarter is worth 25 cents. 10 + 20 + 4 + 25 = 59 cents which can be rounded to 60 cents to match one of the provided answer selections.

TEKS Standard §111.5(b)(5)

15. C: Each number is 7 more than the previous number, so adding 7 to the previous number finds the next number. Thus, the fifth number is 256, the sixth number is 263, and the seventh number is 270.

TEKS Standard §111.5(b)(4)(A) and (4)(K) and (5)

16. B: The farmer plants 17 rows of corn each season. This can be found using all of the information given in the table. The farmer had planted 34 rows of corn by the end of Season 2 and 68 rows of corn by the end of Season 4, indicating an increase of 34 rows of corn between the two seasons. So, by dividing 34 by 2, the numbers of rows planted in one season is found. Also, the farmer had planted 102 rows of corn by the end of Season 6 and 119 rows of corn by the end of Season 7, indicating an increase of 17 rows of corn planted in one season. If 17 rows of corn are added to the number given at the end of Season 2, the result is 51 rows of corn planted by the end of Season 3. If another 17 rows of corn are added to this amount, the farmer would have planted 68 ears of corn by the end of Season 4, which he did. Thus, he did plant 17 rows of corn each year. He had planted 136 rows of corn by the end of Season 8, 153 rows of corn by the end of Season 9, and 170 rows of corn by the end of Season 10.

TEKS Standard §111.5(b)(1)(E)

17. A: A unicycle has only one wheel; uni = one. A bicycle has two wheels; bi = two. A tricycle has three wheels; tri = three. Only answer choice A shows this correct comparison.

TEKS Standard §111.5(b)(5)(B)

18. B: A number sentence that subtracts the number of friends from the total number of stamps will not provide the number of stamps needed to give each friend. Instead, an appropriate multiplication or division number sentence within the following fact family is needed: $9 \times 5 = 45$, $5 \times 9 = 45$, $45 \div 9 = 5$, or $45 \div 5 = 9$.

TEKS Standard §111.5(b)(5)

19. D: The pattern displayed is an arrow pointing right, left, up, right, left....so the next arrow should be pointing up to continue the pattern.

TEKS Standard §111.5(b)(5)

20. B: The number of blocks used in each tower increases by 2. Therefore, the number of blocks used in the next four towers can be found by adding 2 to the number of blocks in the 4th tower and continuing to add 2 blocks for each tower that comes next. This gives: 10, 12, 14, and 16, with 16 blocks used in the eighth tower.

TEKS Standard §111.5(b)(5) and (4)(K)

21. D: The number of books brought by 2 students is 8, while the number of books brought by 5 students and 6 students increased by 4. Thus, the number of books brought by each student was 4. This fact can be checked by starting with 1 student and 4 books brought, and continuing the pattern to make sure it corresponds with the numbers in the table. For example, 8 students brought 32, which does in fact agree with the each student bringing 4 books. So, the number of books each student brought, 4, is multiplied by the number of students to find the total number of books that were brought. Thus, 12 students brought 12 × 4 books, or 48 books.

TEKS Standard §111.5(b)(8)

22. A: Each car has 4 wheels, so the numbers of cars should be multiplied by 4 to find the total number of wheels. 3 cars will have 3 × 4 wheels, or 12 wheels, 4 cars will have 4 × 4 wheels, or 16 wheels, 7 cars will have 7 × 4 wheels, or 28 wheels, 11 cars will have 11 × 4 wheels, or 44 wheels, and 12 cars will have 12 × 4 wheels, or 48 wheels.

TEKS Standard §111.5(b)(6)

23. A: A vertex is a point where two or more edges meet. So, a triangular prism (Choice A) has 6 vertices, while a square pyramid (Choice B) has 5 vertices, a triangular pyramid (Choice C) has 4 vertices, and a cube (Choice D) has 8 vertices. Thus, the triangular prism is the only figure with 6 vertices.

TEKS Standard §111.5(b)(6)

24. D: A line of symmetry is a line that can be drawn through a shape such that the remaining part of the shape on either side of the line looks the same, but is reflected. The shape shown is a hexagon, and it has 6 lines of symmetry. An octagon (Choice D) has 8 lines of symmetry, while an equilateral triangle (Choice A) has 3 lines of symmetry, a rhombus (Choice B) has 2 lines of symmetry, and a trapezoid (Choice C) has 1 line of symmetry. So, the only shape with more lines of symmetry than the hexagon is the octagon.

TEKS Standard §111.5(b)(3)(A)

25. C: The number line shows three marks between each whole number, making 4 equal parts between each whole number. Point S is located at $14\frac{1}{2}$ since it is halfway between 14 and 15, or 2 marks to the right of 14, which can also be written as $14\frac{2}{4}$. $14\frac{3}{4}$ is greater than that number. It is easier to see which fraction is greater if the denominators are the same, since then, just the numerators are compared. So, $14\frac{3}{4}$ is $\frac{1}{4}$ more than the number shown on the number line, and this is the only choice that is greater than the value of Point S.

TEKS Standard §111.5(b)(6)

26. B: The figure shown is a square pyramid. It indeed has 5 vertices and 5 faces. It has 8 edges, not 6 edges, so Choice B is the only statement that is not true.

TEKS Standard §111.5(b)(6)

27. C: The triangle shown for Choice C is congruent to the given triangle, since all side lengths and angles are congruent. Basically, the triangles must be the same size to be congruent, but can be flipped or rotated in any way.

TEKS Standard §111.5(b)

28. A: A triangular pyramid (Choice A) has 4 faces, while a triangular prism (Choice B) and a rectangular pyramid (Choice D) both have 5 faces. A cube (Choice C) has 6 faces. Thus, the only figure with less than 5 faces is the triangular pyramid.

TEKS Standard §111.5(b)(6)(A)

29. D: Figures A, B, and C can all be folded in a manner that the squares lay directly on top of each other. This cannot be done with Figure D; therefore, Figure D does not have a line of symmetry.

TEKS Standard §111.5(b)(6)(A)

30. C: A circle is a two-dimensional shape that is not a polygon. It does not have straight sides that meet at vertices. All of the other choices are two-dimensional polygons.

TEKS Standard §111.5(b)(6)(A)

31. D: The shapes all have at least 6 edges, with a triangular pyramid having 6 edges, a triangular prism having 9 edges, and a square pyramid having 8 edges. These shapes are clearly not all pyramids or all prisms, and they do not all have 5 faces (the triangular prism and square pyramid both have 5 faces but the triangular pyramid has only 4 faces). So, Choice D is the only statement common to all of the shapes.

TEKS Standard §111.5(b)(7)(B)

32. B: The perimeter is the sum of the lengths of all five sides, or $5 + 5 + 3 + 3 + 4$, which equals 20. Therefore, the perimeter of the pentagon is 20 cm.

TEKS Standard §111.5(b)(7)(B)

33. B: To find the perimeter of each shape, add up the lengths of all of the sides. The square has four sides of equal length, so it has a perimeter of 16 centimeters, which is larger than the perimeters of the other three shapes. The triangle and rectangle each have a perimeter of 14 centimeters. The hexagon has a perimeter of 12 centimeters.

TEKS Standard §111.5(b)(7)

34. B: The pencil is approximately 3.25 inches, which rounds to 3 inches.

TEKS Standard §111.5(b)(7)

35. C: The width of the notebook can be estimated by marking off lengths that are close to the measurement of a centimeter. The width of the book is slightly less than 5.5 cm, so it is about 5 cm.

TEKS Standard §111.5(b)(6)(D)

36. D: The triangle includes 21 whole square units, plus 7 one-half square units, or $3\frac{1}{2}$ square units. So, 21 square units plus $3\frac{1}{2}$ square units gives a total of $24\frac{1}{2}$ square units.

TEKS Standard §111.5(b)(7)(B)

37. The perimeter of a figure is the sum of all of its sides. Since a rectangle's width and length will be the same on opposite sides, the perimeter of a rectangle can be calculated by using the following formula: perimeter = 2 x width + 2 x length
Using the numbers given in the question:
perimeter = 2 x 7cm + 2 x 9cm)
perimeter = 14cm + 18cm
perimeter = 32cm

TEKS Standard §111.5(b)(7)

38. D: The thermometer shows 4 marks between each whole number, or 5 intervals. This means each interval on the thermometer represents 2 degrees since there are 5 intervals between each difference of 10 degrees. The thermometer reveals a reading at 4 degrees above 70 degrees (2 marks above 70), or 6 degrees below 80 degrees (3 marks below 80). Thus, the temperature outside is 74 degrees Fahrenheit.

TEKS Standard §111.5(b)(7)

39. A: The short hand, or hour hand, is between 10 o'clock and 11 o'clock, revealing that Amanda arrived after 10 o'clock, but before 11 o'clock. It is much closer to the 10, so this indicates the time is much closer to 10 o'clock than 11 o'clock. The long hand, or minute hand, is pointing to the 2, indicating 10 minutes after the hour. This is because for minutes, each number represents 5 minutes; so $2 \times 5 = 10$. So, she arrived at the party at 10:10.

TEKS Standard §111.5(b)(7)

40. B: Since there are sixty minutes in an hour, a "quarter" in time represents 15 minutes. A quarter past three would mean 15 minutes after 3 o'clock or 3:15. Represented on an analog clock, the big hand would be pointing to the three and the small hand pointing just past the three.

TEKS Standard §111.5(b)(8)

41. B: There are 6 yellow cards and 3 red cards. The more cards there are of a certain color, the more likely it is that the color is drawn. With more yellow cards than red cards in the bag, he is more likely to draw a yellow card than a red card. There are more green cards than yellow cards, so he is more likely to draw a green card than a yellow card. There are less yellow cards than blue cards, so he is less likely to draw a yellow card than a blue card. Finally, the number of red, blue, green, and yellow cards are all different – so none of them are equally likely to be drawn compared to another color. Thus, Choice B is the only true statement.

TEKS Standard §111,5(b)(8)

42. A: The pictograph for Choice A reveals that each picture of a cake represents 5 actual cakes. Therefore, the numbers given in the table, divided by 5, should equal the number of cakes represented in the pictograph. The pictograph accurately shows 5 cakes for 25 actual cakes, 3 cakes for 15 actual cakes, 7 cakes for 35 actual cakes, and 4 cakes for 20 actual cakes. This is the only pictograph that represents the correct number of cakes.

TEKS Standard §111.5(b)(8)

43. C: Florida had 20 teachers that attended the event, which is less than the number of teachers who attended the event from each of the other three states. The number of teachers that attended the event from each of the other states were 40 (Arizona), 80 (New York), and 50 (California). Also, just looking at the bar graph shows that Florida had the least number of teachers attend compared to the other states because the bar is much lower in the graph.

TEKS Standard §111.5(b)(8)

44. D: Since the spinner only has sections, labeled 1 - 8, there is not a section, labeled "9". Therefore, it is impossible for the spinner to land on a 9.

TEKS Standard §111.5(b)(8)

45. C: The more candy there is of a certain kind, the more likely it is that the candy is drawn. With more lollipops than chocolates in the bowl, she is more likely to draw a lollipop than a chocolate. There are more peppermints than chocolates, so she is more likely to draw a peppermint than a chocolate. There are more peppermints than lollipops, so she is more likely to draw a peppermint than a lollipop. Finally, the number of chocolates, peppermints, and lollipops are all different - so none of them are equally likely to be drawn compared to another color. Thus, Choice C is the only true statement.

TEKS Standard §111.5(b)(8)

46. The hamster received 10 votes and the fish received 2 votes. The difference is 10 - 2 = 8 votes.

Additional Bonus Material

Due to our efforts to try to keep this book to a manageable length, we've created a link that will give you access to all of your additional bonus material.

Please visit http://www.mometrix.com/bonus948/staarg3math to access the information.